Healthy Breakfast

TARLA DALAL
India's #1 Cookery Author

D1716368

S&C
SANJAY & CO.
MUMBAI

Seventh Printing : 2006

Copyright © Sanjay & Co.

ISBN : 81-86469-81-8

Price: Rs. 89/-

Published & Distributed by : **Sanjay & Company**

353/A-1, Shah & Nahar Industrial Estate, Dhanraj Mill Compound,
Lower Parel (W), Mumbai - 400 013. INDIA.
Tel. : (91-22) 2496 8068 ● Fax : (91-22) 2496 5876 ● E-mail : sanjay@tarladalal.com

Printed by : **Minal Sales Agencies**, Mumbai

Recipe Research & Production Design	**Nutritionist**	**Photography**	**Design**
Pinky Chandan Dixit	Nisha Katira	Jignesh Jhaveri	Satyamangal Rege
Arati Fedane	**Food Stylist**	**Typesetting**	
Pradnya Sundararaj	Shubhangi Dahimade	Adityas Enterprises	

DISCLAMIER

While every precaution has been taken in the preparation of this book, the publishers and the author assume no responsibility for errors or omissions. Neither is any liability assumed for damages resulting from the use of information contained herein. And of course, no book is a substitute for a qualified medical advice. So it is wiser to modify your dietary patterns under the supervision of a doctor or a nutritionist.

BULK PURCHASES

Tarla Dalal Cookbooks are ideal gifts. If you are interested in buying more than 500 assorted copies of Tarla Dalal Cookbooks at special prices, please contact us at 91-22-2496 8068 or email : sanjay@tarladalal.com

INTRODUCTION

*T*he saying *"Have breakfast like a king, lunch like a prince and dinner like a pauper"* is completely true. Breakfast is your start of the day and as the name suggests it is necessary o "break" the "fast" that has been going on since dinner the previous night to fuel your body or the day. A good breakfast keeps you energetic and healthy as it provides the necessary nutrient boost and prevents bingeing on high calorie foods in latter part of the day.

Healthy Breakfast, my latest addition to *Total Health Series,* comprises of **54 sumptuous breakfast ideas.** All the recipes in this book are made with commonly available ingredients. Care has been taken to avoid high fat, processed and refined foods and use low calorie natural variants instead. Recipes have been compiled using combinations of fruits and vegetables with cereals and pulses and minimal use of fat.

On days when you are on the go, try recipes from the section *Breakfast in a Jiffy* or *Breakfast Using Left-overs.* When you have the time to do that little bit extra to make your breakfast special, make a couple of things from the section *Breakfast with Planning.* Also included are sections on *Healthy Drinks, Butter Substitutes* and *Salt Substitutes.*

Turn to this book to add more colour, flavour, nourishment and variety to the most important meal of the day and ensure good health for the day and ever..... not just for yourself but for your entire family.

Happy Cooking,

Tarla Dalal

CONTENTS

BREAKFAST PLATTER

A great start to any breakfast. This combination of almonds, walnuts, black currants, dates, amla and tulsi is a great start for your breakfast as it enhances the reserves of proteins, fatty acids, vitamin C etc. in your body. You are thus rejuvenated and pepped up to start your day.

This platter is a must for both the young and the old as it not only helps build immunity and resistance to ailments, but also inhibits its progression.

Here's sharing the benefits of each ingredient of this platter in detail.

1 Soaked Almond – Almonds provide some essential fatty acids, which are not produced in our body, along with proteins. They are also well proven as memory enhancers and hence are apt for people of all age groups.

1 Soaked Walnut – Walnuts, a good source of magnesium and certain essential amino acids, have been recently proven to keep the lining of the heart in good health and thus help in maintaining its healthy functioning.

2 to 3 Black Currants and 1 Black Date – Black currants along with dates prevents constipation and stomach upsets and indirectly also have a hand in glowing complexion as they help ward of pimples formed as a result of indigestion.

1 Amla – Amla has been ranked as one of the top rankers among the fruits. 1 amla a day is enough to fulfill your whole day's requirement for vitamin C which helps to build up your immunity and fight against diseases.

2 Tulsi Leaves – Tulsi leaves when consumed everyday helps to fight against the odds of viruses and bacteria and prevents the onset of common ailments like cough, cold, sore throat etc.

· BROKEN WHEAT UPMA ·

Picture on cover

A broken wheat variation of the traditional semolina upma. The carrots and green peas add the necessary crunch along with the wealth of vitamin A.

Preparation time : 15 minutes.   Cooking time : 20 minutes.   Serves 4.

½ cup broken wheat (bulgur wheat)
½ cup onions, chopped
1 green chilli, chopped
½ tsp grated ginger
¼ cup green peas
¼ cup carrots, diced
¼ tsp mustard seeds (rai)
2 tsp oil
salt to taste

For the garnish
2 tbsp chopped coriander

9

1. Clean and wash the broken wheat thoroughly. Drain and keep aside.
2. Heat the oil in a pressure cooker. Add the mustard seeds.
3. When they cackle, add the onions, green chilli and ginger and sauté till the onions turn translucent.
4. Add the green peas, carrots, broken wheat and salt and sauté for 3 to 4 minutes.
5. Add 1½ cups of water and pressure cook for 1 whistle.
   Garnish with the coriander and serve hot.

Nutritive values per serving
Energy : 107 calories.
Protein : 2.4 gm.
Carbohydrate : 18.0 gm.
Fat : 2.8 gm.
Vitamin A : 199.7 mcg.

· CUCUMBER PANCAKES ·

T ry one and you are sure to opt for a second helping of this cucumber semolina pancake.

Preparation time : 5 minutes.   Cooking time : 20 minutes.   Makes 8 pancakes.

cups semolina (rawa)
cups cucumber, grated
tbsp grated jaggery (gur)
green chilli, chopped
4 cup low fat curds (yoghurt), page 101
alt to taste

Other ingredients
tsp oil for cooking

For serving
tbsp nutritious green chutney, page 98

11

1. Combine all the ingredients except the oil and make a batter of dropping consistency using a little water.
2. Divide into 8 portions and keep aside.
3. Heat a non-stick pan and grease it lightly with oil.
4. Spread one portion on the non-stick pan to make a pancake of 3 mm. to 4 mm. thickness.
5. Cook one side over a slow flame until the base is golden brown in colour. Turn over to cook the other side.
6. Remove the pancake and repeat with the remaining batter to make 7 more pancakes. Serve hot with nutritious green chutney.

Nutritive values per pancake
Energy : 130 calories.
Protein : 3.5 gm.
Carbohydrate : 22.2 gm.
Fat : 2.8 gm.
Calcium : 63.9 gm.

· NUTRITIOU/ CHILA ·

T his yummy chila is made using maize, jowar and whole wheat flour. You could use any combination of flours from your kitchen shelf.

Preparation time : 4 minutes.   Cooking time : 10 minutes.   Makes 4 chilas.

3 tbsp maize flour (makai ka atta)
3 tbsp jowar flour (white millet flour)
3 tbsp wheat flour (gehun ka atta)
¼ cup onions, chopped
½ cup tomato, chopped
2 tbsp chopped coriander
2 green chillies, finely chopped
salt to taste

Other ingredients
tsp oil for cooking

For serving
oriander garlic chutney, page 96

13

1. Mix together all the ingredients in a bowl and add enough water to make a soft loose dough. Divide into 4 equal parts.
2. Heat a non-stick pan and grease it lightly with oil.
3. Spread a layer of the batter to form a pancake of 4 mm. thickness.
4. Cook on both sides till golden brown, using a little oil.
5. Repeat with the remaining batter to make 3 more chilas.
   Serve hot with coriander garlic chutney.

Nutritive values per chila
Energy : 68 calories.
Protein : 1.9 gm.
Carbohydrate : 11.6 gm.
Fat : 1.6 gm.
Vitamin A : 189.3 mcg.
Fibre : 0.5 mg.

· SOYA UPMA ·

A good example of a famous Indian breakfast made with a slight modification by the addition of soya granules for an iron and protein boost. Try it, I am sure you can easily adapt this healthy change.

Preparation time : 20 minutes.   Cooking time : 10 minutes.   Serves 4.

¼ cup soya granules
1 tsp cumin seeds (jeera)
1 tbsp urad dal (split black lentils)
¼ tsp asafoetida (hing)
. tsp grated ginger
 to 2 green chillies, slit
½ cup onions, chopped
½ cup carrots, grated
½ cup cabbage, chopped
2 tsp oil
salt to taste

For the garnish
2 tbsp chopped coriander
4 lemon wedges

1. Soak the soya granules in hot water for approx. 15 minutes. Drain, squeeze out all the water and keep aside. Discard the water.
2. Heat the oil in a non-stick pan and add the cumin seeds. When they crackle, add the urad dal and sauté till the dal turns light brown.
3. Add the asafoetida, ginger, green chillies and onions.
4. Sauté the onions till they are translucent. Add the carrots and cabbage and sauté for 4 to 5 minutes.
5. Add the soya granules and mix well.
6. Season with salt and mix well.
   Serve hot garnished with the coriander and lemon wedges.

Nutritive values per serving
Energy : 96 calories.
Protein : 5.5 gm.
Carbohydrate : 8.2 gm.
Fat : 4.5 gm.
Iron : 1.5 mg.

• SPICED WHOLEMEAL AND OAT PANCAKES •

Picture on page 19

A healthy version of the traditional pancakes which are made of plain flour (maida).

Preparation time : 5 minutes.   Cooking time : 10 minutes.   Makes 6 pancakes.

cup whole wheat flour (gehun ka atta)
cup quick cooking rolled oats
pinch nutmeg (jaiphal) powder
pinch cardamom (elaichi) powder
tsp cinnamon (dalchini) powder
tbsp powdered sugar
sp oil
cup low fat milk, page 101
tsp Eno's fruit salt
pinch of salt

Other ingredients
3 tsp low fat butter for cooking

For serving
2 tbsp honey
½ cup orange segments

1. Combine all the ingredients except the fruit salt in a bowl with enough water.
2. Whisk till it is a smooth batter.
3. Heat a non-stick pan and grease it with a little low fat butter.
4. Add the fruit salt to the batter and mix well. Divide into 6 equal portions.
5. Pour a spoonful of the batter on the pan to make 50 mm. (2") diameter pancake, cooking on both sides with a little butter till golden brown.
6. Repeat with the remaining batter to make 5 more pancakes.
   Serve hot with honey and oranges.

Nutritive values per pancake
Energy : 109 calories.
Protein : 2.9 gm.
Carbohydrate : 19.6 gm.
Fat : 2.4 gm.
Calcium : 33.6 mg.

Spiced Wholemeal and Oat Pancakes : Recipe on page 17

· BATATA POHA ·

*T his traditional Maharashtrian recipe is made of iron-rich poha. Don't forget to serve
it with lemon wedges as it is the vitamin C present in lemons that aids the absorption of iron
form the poha.*

Preparation time : 10 minutes.   Cooking time : 10 minutes.   Serves 4.

2 cups thick poha (beaten rice flakes)
½ tsp mustard seeds (rai)
½ tsp cumin seeds (jeera)
6 to 8 curry leaves
3 to 4 green chillies, slit
½ cup onions, chopped
½ cup potato, peeled and cubed
¼ tsp turmeric powder (haldi)
1 tsp sugar (optional)
2 tsp oil
salt to taste

For the garnish
2 tbsp chopped coriander
4 lemon wedges

1. Place the poha in a sieve and hold it under running water for a few seconds. Toss well to drain out all excess water and keep aside.
2. Heat the oil in a non-stick pan and add the mustard seeds and cumin seeds.
3. When the seeds crackle, add the curry leaves and green chillies and stir for 1 minute.
4. Add the onions and sauté till the onions turn golden brown.
5. Add the potato, turmeric powder, salt and a little water. Cover and heat on medium flame till the potatoes are cooked.
6. Add the poha, sugar and a little more salt and mix well.
   Serve hot garnished with the coriander and lemon wedges.

Handy tip : If the poha gets too dry sprinkle a tbsp milk, mix well and serve immediately.

Nutritive values per serving
Energy : 150 calories.
Protein : 2.5 gm.
Carbohydrate : 28.5 gm.
Fat : 3.0 gm.
Iron : 6.2 mg.
Vitamin C : 7.7 mg.

· BANANA APPLE PORRIDGE ·

 BREAKFAST in a JIFFY

Picture on page 37

A wholesome broken wheat and oat porridge served with apples and bananas.

Preparation time : 5 minutes.   Cooking time : 10 minutes.   Serves 4.

¼ cup broken wheat (bulgur wheat)
¼ cup quick cooking rolled oats
1 cup low fat milk, page 101
1 tbsp powdered sugar
½ tsp cinnamon (dalchini) powder
1½ cups apple, diced
3 cups bananas, sliced
4 tsp low fat butter

For the garnish
4 cinnamon (dalchini) sticks (optional)

1. Clean, wash and drain the broken wheat.
2. Heat the butter in a pressure cooker, add the broken wheat and sauté for 3 to 4 minutes.
3. Add the oats and cook for 2 minutes.

2

4. Add the milk and 1 cup of water and pressure cook for 2 whistles.
5. Mix in the sugar and cinnamon powder. Cool in the refrigerator.
6. Add the apples and bananas. Mix well.
   Serve chilled garnished with cinnamon sticks.

Nutritive values per serving
Energy : 260 calories.
Protein : 5.0 gm.
Carbohydrate : 53.4 gm.
Fat : 2.9 gm.
Calcium : 97.9 mg.

· SOYA KHAMAN DHOKLA ·

T ry this healthy version of dhokla made with a combination of Bengal gram flour and soya flour for an "iron kick".

Preparation time : 5 minutes.   Cooking time : 10 minutes.   Serves 6.

For the batter
¾ cup Bengal gram flour (besan)
¼ cup soya flour
1½ tbsp semolina (rawa)
½ tsp citric acid (nimbu ke phool)
3½ tsp sugar
1 tsp green chilli-ginger paste
1½ tsp Eno's fruit salt
salt to taste

For the tempering
½ tsp mustard seeds (rai)
½ tsp sesame seeds (til)
2 green chillies, chopped
a pinch asafoetida (hing)
2 tsp oil

For the garnish
1 tbsp chopped coriander

For serving
nutritious green chutney, page 98

1. Mix together all the ingredients for the batter, except the fruit salt, using enough water to make a thick batter.
2. Add in the fruit salt, sprinkle a little water over the fruit salt and mix well. The mixture will rise immediately.
3. When the mixture rises, pour it into a greased thali and steam for about 10 minutes.
4. For the tempering, heat the oil in a small pan and add the mustard seeds, sesame seeds, green chillies and asafoetida. When the mustard seeds crackle, add 1 tbsp of water and pour this over the steamed dhoklas.
5. Cut into pieces and serve hot with nutritious green chutney.

Handy tips : 1. You can use 1 tsp of lemon juice instead of the citric acid crystals.
2. Keep the steamer hot and only then add the fruit salt into the batter.

Nutritive values per serving
Energy : 87 calories.
Protein : 3.7 gm.
Carbohydrate : 11.8 gm.
Fat : 2.8 gm.
Iron : 1.0 mg.

• MUESLI •

This combination of cereals and nuts is a complete breakfast in itself. It does not have to be accompanied by any juice, milk or fruit.

Preparation time : 5 minutes.   Cooking time : 10 minutes.   Serves 4.

1 cup quick rolled cooking oats
4 tbsp wheat bran
2 tbsp chopped walnuts
2 tbsp chopped almonds
2 cups cornflakes
¼ tsp vanilla essence
3 tbsp sultanas (kismis)

For serving
4 cups warm low fat milk, page 101
1½ cups apple (unpeeled), chopped
1 cup banana, chopped
1 tsp sugar

1. Combine the oats, wheat bran, walnuts and almonds and lightly roast them in a non-stick pan over a slow flame for 5 to 7 minutes.
2. Cool completely, add the cornflakes, vanilla essence and sultanas. Mix well.
3. Store in an air-tight container.
4. For serving, place the muesli into individual bowls with sugar, apple and banana and pour warm milk.
   Serve immediately.

Nutritive values per serving
Energy : 281 calories.
Protein : 13.2 gm.
Carbohydrate : 51.6 gm.
Fat : 2.3 gm.
Iron : 3.9 mg.
Folic Acid : 38.2 mcg.
Calcium : 308.9 mg.

· VEGETABLE GRILLED SANDWICH ·

*B*rown bread sliced stuffed with cabbage, carrot and cheese. A hearty cold-weather pleaser, appropriate to keep you going on busy days with late lunches.

Preparation time : 10 minutes.　　Cooking time : 10 minutes.　　Makes 4 sandwiches.

8 slices whole wheat bread

For the stuffing
¾ cup cabbage, shredded
¾ cup carrots, thickly grated
¾ cup low fat paneer (cottage cheese), page 102, grated
2 tbsp chopped coriander
1 green chilli, chopped
2 tbsp mozzarella cheese
salt to taste

Other ingredients
4 tsp low fat butter for cooking

For the stuffing

Mix all the ingredients together. Divide the stuffing into 4 equal portions.

How to proceed

1. Place one portion of the stuffing on one slice of bread. Top with another slice of bread.
2. Repeat with the remaining ingredients to make 3 more sandwiches.
3. Pre-heat the griller and grill the sandwiches, using a little low fat butter to cook. Serve hot.

Nutritive values per sandwich

Energy : 224 calories.
Protein : 9.0 gm.
Carbohydrate : 25.0 gm.
Fat : 9.8 gm.
Vitamin A : 545.3 mcg.
Calcium : 194.4 mg.

• JOWAR PYAZ KI ROTI •

*J*owar rotis flavoured with spring onions and green chilli.

Preparation time : 5 minutes.   Cooking time : 20 minutes.   Makes 4 rotis.

1 cup jowar flour (white millet flour)
1 spring onion, finely chopped
1 green chilli, finely chopped
2 tsp oil
salt to taste

For serving
chunky vegetable spread, page 93

1. Combine all the ingredients in a bowl and knead into a soft dough,
   using warm water as required.
2. Cover and keep aside for 10 minutes.
3. Divide the dough into 4 equal portions.

4. Pat each portion on a dry surface using your palm till it is a circle of 125 mm. (5")
   diameter.
5. Cook on a non-stick pan with a little oil till both sides are lightly browned.
   Serve hot with chunky vegetable spread.

Handy tip : If you want to roll out these rotis, you can do so between 2 sheets of plastic.

Nutritive values per roti
Energy : 113 calories.
Protein : 2.7 gm.
Carbohydrate : 18.8 gm.
Fat : 3.3 gm.

· MINI SOYA DOSA ·

*D*osa made with the soya milk and wheat flour to make up for your vitamin A and calcium
requirement.

Preparation time : 2 minutes.   Cooking time : 15 minutes.   Makes 6 dosas.

1 cup soya milk
¼ cup whole wheat flour (gehun ka atta)
1 green chilli, chopped
½ cup onions, grated
1 tbsp chopped coriander
¼ tsp Eno's fruit salt
salt to taste
1½ tsp oil for cooking

For serving
garlic tomato chutney, page 94

1. Make a thin batter using the soya milk, wheat flour, green chilli, onions, coriander,
   fruit salt, salt and water. Mix well.

Heat a non-stick pan and grease it with a little oil.
Pour 2 tbsp of the batter on the non-stick pan and spread it using a circular motion to make a thin dosa.
Cook on both sides using a little oil.
Repeat with the remaining batter to make 5 more dosas.
Serve hot with garlic tomato chutney.

Nutritive values per dosa
Energy : 59 calories.
Protein : 1.9 gm.
Carbohydrate : 7.3 gm.
Fat : 2.4 gm.
Calcium : 47.6 mg.
Vitamin A : 125.4 mcg.

• CORN PANKI •

*C*orn and semolina pancakes cooked between circles of banana leaves. Accompanied with a tall glass of milkshake, this truly is a healthy breakfast.

Preparation time : 5 minutes.   Cooking time : 20 minutes.   Makes 16 pankis.

2 nos. corn cobs, grated
3 tbsp semolina (rawa)
2 tsp chopped coriander
1 tsp finely chopped green chillies
1 tbsp fresh low fat curds (yoghurt), page 101
1 tsp oil
salt to taste

Other ingredients
3 banana leaves
oil for greasing

arrot garlic chutney, page 97

. Using a 75 mm. (3") diameter cookie cutter, cut out 32 rounds of the banana leaves. Grease the banana leaf rounds with some oil and keep aside.
. In a bowl, combine the corn, semolina, coriander, green chillies, curds, oil, salt and 1/3 cup of water and mix well.
. Heat a tava (griddle) and place 4 greased banana leaf rounds on it.
. Pour a spoonful of the corn mixture on each banana leaf round and cover with another greased banana leaf round. Cook on both sides till the banana leaves brown slightly and the pancake in-between peels off the banana leaf easily.
. Repeat twice to make 12 more pankis.
  Serve hot with the carrot garlic chutney.

utritive values per panki
nergy : 30 calories.
rotein : 0.9 gm.
arbohydrate : 6.1 gm.
at : 0.5 gm.
bre : 0.5 gm.

• SPICY SPROUTS SANDWICH •

E *legant sandwiches with a sprout and potato stuffing instead of cheese to enhance your calcium and fibre levels.*

Preparation time : 10 minutes.   Cooking time : 20 minutes.   Makes 4 sandwiches.

8 slices whole wheat bread
½ cup onions, sliced
4 tsp low fat butter to cook

For the sprouts
1 cup mixed sprouts, boiled
½ cup potatoes, boiled and mashed
½ cup onions, finely chopped
2 tsp ginger-garlic paste
1 green chilli, finely chopped
2 tsp pav bhaji masala

Banana Apple Porridge : Recipe on page 22

2 tsp coriander-cumin seed (dhania-jeera) powder
¼ tsp turmeric powder (haldi)
½ tsp black salt (sanchal)
1½ cups tomatoes, finely chopped
2 tsp oil
salt to taste

For the sprouts
1. Heat the oil in a non-stick pan, add the onions and sauté till the onions turn translucent.
2. Add the ginger-garlic paste, green chilli and sauté for another 1 minute.
3. Add the pav bhaji masala, coriander-cumin seed powder, turmeric powder, black salt, tomatoes and salt and cook for 5 minutes.
4. Add the sprouts and potatoes and mix well. Keep aside.

How to proceed
1. Divide the sprouts mixture into 4 equal portions.
2. Place one portion on one slice of bread. Top with an onion slice and sandwich using another slice of bread.
3. Repeat with the remaining ingredients to make 3 more sandwiches.
4. Pre-heat the griller and grill the sandwiches, using a little low fat butter to cook. Serve hot.

Handy tip : Pav bhaji masala is a spice blend that is easily available at provision stores.

Nutritive values per sandwich
Energy : 220 calories.
Protein : 8.4 gm.
Carbohydrate : 34.7 gm.
Fat : 5.2 gm.
Calcium : 81.0 mg.
Fibre : 1.8 mg.

· CREAMY SPINACH TOAST ·

A classic fixture for the breakfast menu on days when you are on go.

Preparation time : 15 minutes.   Cooking time : 15 minutes.   Makes 30 pieces.
Baking time : 5 mins.   Baking temperature : 200°C (400°F).

For the toast
10 slices whole wheat bread

For the spinach stuffing
3 cups spinach (palak), chopped
½ cup onions, chopped
2 green chillies, finely chopped
a pinch soda bi-carb
¾ cup low fat milk, page 101
2 tsp cornflour
1 tbsp low fat butter
salt to taste

For the topping
3 tbsp grated cheese
Tabasco sauce (optional)

For the spinach stuffing
1. Heat the butter in a non-stick pan, add the onions and sauté till the onions turn translucent. Add the green chillies and fry again for a few seconds.
2. Add the spinach and soda bi-carb and cook for 2 minutes.
3. Mix the milk with the cornflour. Add to the mixture and cook until the mixture becomes thick. Add salt and mix well. Keep aside.

How to proceed
1. Cut each bread slice into three long strips and toast them.
2. Spread a little spinach mixture on each toast piece.
3. Sprinkle some grated cheese on top.
4. Grill in a hot oven at 200°C (400°F) for a few minutes, so as to melt the cheese. Serve hot with Tabasco sauce.

Nutritive values per piece
Energy : 32 calories.
Protein : 1.2 gm.
Carbohydrate : 4.1 gm.
Fat : 1.1 gm.
Vitamin A : 393.3 mcg.
Calcium : 25.0 mg.

• RICE AND MOONG DAL IDLI •

The rice and dal combination of this idli in quite nutritious as it provides complete protein.

Preparation time : 20 minutes.   Cooking time : 15 minutes.   Makes 6 idlis.

½ cup rice
½ cup moong dal (split green gram)
¼ tsp fenugreek (methi) seeds (optional)
½ cup carrots, grated
½ cup spring onion whites and greens, finely chopped
a pinch soda bi-carb
salt to taste

For serving
nutritious green chutney, page 98

1. Soak the rice, moong dal and fenugreek seeds in water for 5 to 6 hours.
2. Grind the soaked ingredients in a mixer and leave the batter aside to ferment for at least 8 hours or preferably overnight.

3. Thereafter, add the soda bi-carb, carrots, spring onion whites, spring onion greens and salt and mix well.
4. Pour the mixture into greased idli moulds.
5. Steam in a steamer for a few minutes, till they are done.
   Serve hot with nutritious green chutney.

Handy tip : The idli is done when a toothpick or a knife inserted in its center comes out clean.

Nutritive values per idli
Energy : 95 calories.
Protein : 4.2 gm.
Carbohydrate : 19.1 gm.
Fat : 0.2 gm.
Vitamin A : 160.8 mcg.
Folic Acid : 20.6 mcg.

· STUFFED MOONG SPROUTS DOSA ·

A filling breakfast that provides a good wallop of protein (for healthy cells), calcium (for healthy bones) and iron (for good hemoglobin). Great way to eat sprouts for those who don't like it.

Preparation time : 20 minutes.   Cooking time : 20 minutes.   Makes 4 dosas.

For the dosas
1 cup moong sprouts
4 tbsp rice flour
salt to taste

For the stuffing
½ potato, boiled and mashed
2 tbsp grated carrot
2 tbsp grated beetroot
2 tbsp grated cabbage
2 tbsp finely chopped onions
¼ cup tomato, finely chopped
1 tbsp chopped coriander
½ tsp chaat masala

¼ tsp mustard seeds (rai)
2 curry leaves
a pinch turmeric powder (haldi)
a pinch asafoetida (hing)
1 tsp oil
salt to taste

Other ingredients
1 tsp oil to cook

For serving
coriander garlic chutney, page 96

For the dosa
1. Combine the sprouts with ¾ cup of water in a blender and grind into a smooth paste.
2. Add the rice flour and salt and mix well so that no lumps remain. Allow the batter to stand for 15 minutes. Add more water if required to adjust the consistency of the batter so that it is of dropping consistency.

For the stuffing
Heat the oil in a non-stick pan and add the mustard seeds, curry leaves and turmeric powder.

2. When the mustard seeds crackle, add the asafoetida. Add all the vegetables, coriander, chaat masala and salt and mix well.
3. Divide the filling mixture into 4 equal portions. Keep aside.

How to proceed
1. Heat and grease a non-stick pan with a little oil.
2. Pour a ladleful of the batter on the non-stick pan and spread it evenly using a circular motion.
3. Drizzle a little oil on the sides and allow to cook.
4. Top with one portion of the filling mixture and spread it evenly over the dosa.
5. When the lower side of the dosa is lightly browned, fold over.
6. Repeat to make 3 more dosas.
   Serve hot with coriander garlic chutney.

Nutritive values per dosa
Energy : 126 calories.
Protein : 5.0 gm.
Carbohydrate : 20.3 gm.
Fat : 2.8 gm.
Calcium : 37.6 mg.
Iron : 1.1 mg.

• HARI CHILA ROTI •

T hese whole wheat rotis are enriched with spinach, fenugreek and coriander mixture and garnished with bean sprouts, tomatoes and cheese for enhanced taste and vitamins.

Preparation time : 15 minutes.   Cooking time : 10 minutes.   Makes 4 rotis.

For the dough
¾ cup whole wheat flour (gehun ka atta)
½ green chilli, finely chopped
⅓ cup low fat curds (yoghurt), page 101
salt to taste

For the hara chila mixture
2 tbsp chopped fenugreek (methi) leaves
2 tbsp chopped spinach (palak) leaves
2 tbsp chopped fresh coriander
½ green chilli, finely chopped
1 tbsp Bengal gram flour (besan)
salt to taste

For the garnish
2 tbsp bean sprouts
2 tbsp chopped tomatoes
2 tsp grated cheese

Other ingredients
2 tsp oil for cooking

For the dough
1. Combine all the ingredients and knead into a soft dough using a little water if required.
2. Divide into 4 equal portions and keep aside.

For the hara chila mixture
Combine all the ingredients with $\frac{1}{3}$ cup water and mix well. Keep aside.

How to proceed
1. Roll out each portion of the dough into circle of 100 mm. (4") diameter.
2. Place all 4 rotis on a large non-stick pan and cook using a little oil till one side is slightly cooked.
3. Upturn the rotis and spoon out the chila mixture on them.
4. Top with the bean spouts, tomatoes and cheese.
5. Cook on both sides using a little oil.

Serve hot.

Nutritive values per roti
Energy : 168 calories.
Protein : 6.2 gm.
Carbohydrate : 20.8 gm.
Fat : 5.8 gm.
Vitamin A : 621.3 mcg.
Calcium : 117.0 mg.

· PALAK METHI MUTHIA ·

T *hese spinach and fenugreek dumplings make delicious treats for kids. They can munch on this finger-food and get a little nourishment at the same time.*

Preparation time : 10 minutes.   Cooking time : 25 minutes.   Serves 4.

For the muthias
3 cups spinach (palak), finely chopped
1½ cups fenugreek (methi) leaves, finely chopped
1 tsp green chilli-ginger paste
2 tbsp whole wheat flour (gehun ka atta)
1 tbsp Bengal gram flour (besan)
1 tbsp semolina (rawa)
½ tsp cumin seeds (jeera)
a pinch soda bi-carb
2 tsp sugar
1 tbsp lemon juice
1 tsp oil
salt to taste
oil for greasing

For the tempering
1 tsp mustard seeds (rai)
1 tsp sesame seeds (til)
¼ tsp asafoetida (hing)
1 tsp oil

For serving
nutritious green chutney, page 98

For the muthias
1. Combine the spinach and fenugreek leaves with 1 tsp of salt and keep aside for about 5 minutes.
2. Squeeze out all the liquid and place the spinach and fenugreek leaves in a bowl.
3. Add all the remaining ingredients (other than for the tempering) and knead to a very soft dough adding 1 to 2 tbsp of water if required.
4. Apply a little oil on your hands and divide the mixture into 4 equal portions. Shape each portion into a cylindrical roll approx. 150 mm. (6") length and 25 mm. (1") in diameter.
5. Steam in a steamer till done.
6. Cut into 12 mm. (½") slices and keep aside.

How to proceed

1. For the tempering, heat the oil in a large pan and add the mustard seeds and sesame seeds. When the seeds crackle, add the asafoetida.
2. Add the sliced muthias, toss well and stir over gentle heat for 2 to 3 minutes till they are lightly browned.
3. Serve hot with nutritious green chutney.

Handy tips : It will take approx. 20 minutes on a medium flame for the muthias to be cooked till done.

To check if the muthias are done, insert a toothpick in the centre. If it come out clean, the muthias are cooked.

Nutritive values per serving

Energy : 94 calories.
Protein : 3.0 gm.
Carbohydrate : 9.7 gm.
Fat : 4.8 gm.
Vitamin A : 747.6 mcg.

· MOOLI PARATHAS ·

Picture on page 55

*T*his traditional Gujarati delicacy has a shelf life of about 5 days even at room temperature.

Preparation time : 5 minutes.   Cooking time : 25 minutes.   Makes 15 parathas.

cups whole wheat flour (gehun ka atta)
4 cup white radish (mooli), grated
4 cup radish (mooli) leaves, finely chopped
4 cup fresh low fat curds (yoghurt), page 101
2 tsp turmeric powder (haldi)
½ tsp chilli powder
tsp oil
lt to taste

ther ingredients
½ tbsp oil for cooking

or serving
rsley yoghurt spread, page 94

1. Mix all the ingredients and knead into a soft dough, adding a little water if required.
2. Divide the dough into 15 equal portions.
3. Roll out each portion thinly into a 125 mm. (5") diameter circle.
4. Cook each paratha on both sides on a non-stick pan, smearing a little oil on each side, until brown spots appear on the surface.
   Serve hot or cold with parsley yoghurt spread.

VARIATION : METHI PARATHAS

You can use chopped fenugreek (methi) leaves instead of radish for the above recipe.

Nutritive values per paratha
Energy : 89 calories.
Protein : 2.3 gm.
Carbohydrate : 10.7 gm.
Fat : 3.9 gm.
Vitamin A : 174.4 mcg.

Mooli Parathas : Recipe on page 53

• MAKAI KA DHOKLA •

*C*elebrate a fibre treat with these scrumptious sweet corn and maize flour dhoklas with coriander garlic chutney.

Preparation time : 30 minutes.   Cooking time : 20 minutes.   Serves 4.

1 cup maize flour (makai ka atta)
½ cup sour low fat curds (yoghurt), page 101
½ cup sweet corn kernels
2 tsp ginger-green chilli paste
¼ tsp asafoetida (hing)
2 tsp sugar
1 tsp lemon juice
1 tsp Eno's fruit salt
1 tsp oil
salt to taste

For the tempering
1 tsp mustard seeds (rai)
1 tsp sesame seeds (til)

pinch asafoetida (hing)
tsp oil

other ingredients
tsp oil for greasing

or the garnish
tbsp chopped coriander

or serving
coriander garlic chutney, page 96

Combine the maize flour and sour curds with ½ cup of warm water in a bowl. Mix well to make a smooth batter. Keep aside for at least 30 minutes.

Add the sweet corn, ginger-green chilli paste, asafoetida, sugar, lemon juice, oil and mix well.

Add the fruit salt, mix gently and pour the batter into a greased 150 mm. (6") diameter thali. Steam for 15 to 20 minutes.

For the tempering heat the oil, add the mustard seeds, sesame seeds and asafoetida and fry till the mustard seeds crackle. Pour the tempering over the prepared dhokla.

Garnish with the chopped coriander, cut into pieces

Serve hot with the coriander garlic chutney.

Nutritive values per serving
Energy : 93 calories.
Protein : 2.7 gm.
Carbohydrate : 13.7 gm.
Fat : 3.4 gm.
Fibre : 1.0 mg.

· SPICY BAJRA ROTI ·

This recipe involves a little extra effort, but the results are well worth it. For a healthy accompaniment, serve it with low fat butter instead of the regular homemade butter.

Preparation time : 10 minutes.   Cooking time : 20 minutes.   Makes 8 rotis.

or the dough
½ cups bajra flour (black millet flour)
pinch salt

o be mixed into a stuffing
cup crumbled low fat paneer (cottage cheese), page 102
tbsp chopped fenugreek (methi) leaves
green chilli, finely chopped
cup tomatoes, finely chopped
lt to taste

or the cooking
sp low fat butter

For serving
parsley yoghurt spread, page 94

1. For the dough, mix the bajra flour, salt and enough hot water to make a soft dough.
2. Knead well, divide into 16 portions and roll out each portion into thin rotis.
3. To proceed, spread a little stuffing on one roti. Then put another roti on top and press well so that it becomes one roti. Repeat for the remaining rotis and stuffing to make 7 more stuffed rotis.
4. Cook each stuffed roti on a non-stick pan on both sides with a little low fat butter till brown spots appear.
   Serve hot with parsley yoghurt spread.

Nutritive values per roti
Energy : 134 calories.
Protein : 5.1 gm.
Carbohydrate : 22.9 gm.
Fat : 2.4 gm.
Calcium : 67.1 mg.
Iron : 2.5 mg.

· NACHNI PANCAKES ·

The secret of this savoury pancakes is the use of ragi flour spiced with ginger and green chillies.

Preparation time : 15 minutes.   Cooking time : 20 minutes.   Makes 6 pancakes.

1 cup ragi (nachni) flour
1 tbsp soya flour
1 tsp sesame seeds (til)
½ cup onions, grated
2 green chillies, finely chopped
1 tsp grated ginger
½ cup coriander, chopped
salt to taste
2 tsp oil for cooking

For serving
carrot garlic chutney, page 97

1. In a bowl, combine the ragi flour, soya flour, sesame seeds, onions, green chillies, ginger, coriander and salt and mix well with a little water to make a smooth loose dough. Divide into 6 portions and keep aside.
2. Heat a non-stick pan and grease it with a little oil.
3. Wet your fingers and spread an even layer of one portion of the dough to make a 125 mm. (5") round.
4. Cook on both sides till golden brown, using a little oil.
5. Repeat with the rest of the batter to make 5 more pancakes.
   Serve hot with the carrot garlic chutney.

Nutritive values per pancake
Energy : 93 calories.
Protein : 2.4 gm.
Carbohydrate : 15.5 gm.
Fat : 2.3 gm.
Calcium : 83.0 mg.
Iron : 1.0 mg.

· SPICY MOONG DAL DHOKLA ·

A quick and appetizing breakfast. All you need to do to make this dish in a jiffy is to soak moong dal in advance.

Preparation time : 10 minutes.   Cooking time : 15 minutes.   Serves 4.

1 cup moong dal (split green gram) with skin
2 to 3 green chillies
2 tbsp chopped fenugreek (methi) leaves
2 tsp Bengal gram flour (besan)
a pinch asafoetida (hing)
¼ tsp soda-bi-carb
2 pinches sugar (optional)
2 tsp oil
salt to taste

For serving
coriander garlic chutney, page 96

63

1. Soak the moong dal in water for 3 to 4 hours. Wash it very well.
2. Blend the soaked dal in a blender with the green chillies and a little water.
3. Add the fenugreek leaves, gram flour, asafoetida, soda bi-carb, sugar, oil and salt and mix well.
4. Grease a thali with a little oil and steam in a steamer for about 20 minutes.
5. Cut into pieces and serve hot with coriander garlic chutney.

Nutritive values per serving
Energy : 129 calories.
Protein : 7.4 gm.
Carbohydrate : 18.2 gm.
Fat : 2.9 gm.
Iron : 1.2 mg.

Crispy Bread Cups : Recipe on page 66 -

• CRISPY BREAD CUPS •

Picture on page 65

A sumptuous bread delight!! These tasty calcium rich cups can equally work well as appetizers to a main meal.

Preparation time : 15 minutes.   Cooking time : 25 minutes.   Makes 8 pieces.
Baking time : 15 to 20 minutes.   Baking temperature : 200°C (400°F).

For the toast cases
8 slices whole wheat bread
3 tsp low fat butter

For the filling
1½ cups corn, cooked
2 tbsp chopped onions
2 tbsp chopped capsicum
2 tsp finely chopped green chillies
1 cup low fat milk, page 101
1 tbsp cornflour

1 tsp oil
salt to taste

For baking
1 tsp grated cheese

For the toast cases
1. Remove the crust from the bread slices.
2. Wrap the bread slices in a muslin cloth and steam them for 5 to 7 minutes in a pressure cooker.
3. Roll out a little and press into the cavities of a muffin tray which is greased with butter.
4. Brush with melted butter and bake in a hot oven at 200°C (400°F) for 10 minutes or until crisp.

For the filling
1. Heat the oil in a non-stick pan, add the onions and sauté till they are golden brown.
2. Add the capsicum and green chillies and fry for 1 minute.
3. Add the corn, milk, cornflour and salt and cook till the mixture thickens. Keep aside.

How to proceed
Fill a little mixture in each toast case, sprinkle cheese on top. Bake in hot oven at 200°C (400°F) for 5 to 10 minutes or until the cheese melts.
Serve hot.

Nutritive values per piece
Energy : 107 calories.
Protein : 4.3 gm.
Carbohydrate : 17.4 gm.
Fat : 2.2 gm.
Calcium : 53.6 mg.

· WHOLE WHEAT SALAD WRAP ·

T *hese whole-wheat salad wraps are rich in vitamin A, iron, vitamin C and fibre, making a wholesome, satiating breakfast, from left-over chapatis. This dish can be put together quickly, if the hummus has been prepared in advance and refrigerated.*

Preparation time : 4 hours.   Cooking time : 30 minutes.   Makes 4 wraps.

4 left-over whole wheat chapatis, approx. 200 mm. (8") in diameter
1 recipe garlic tomato chutney, page 94

For the salad
½ cup tomatoes, thinly sliced
½ cup spring onions, sliced
½ cup carrot, cut into thin strips
½ cup bean sprouts
1 cup lettuce, shredded
2 tbsp finely chopped coriander
2 tbsp finely chopped mint
½ tsp roasted cumin (jeera) powder
juice of ½ lemon
1 tsp olive oil or oil

salt to taste

For the salad
1. Combine all the vegetables and bean sprouts in a bowl and refrigerate for at least 30 minutes.
2. Just before serving, add the cumin powder, lemon juice, olive oil and salt and mix well.

How to proceed
1. Place one chapati on a clean dry surface.
2. Spread an even layer of the chutney on the chapati.
3. Top with a generous portion of salad in the centre of the chapati and roll up tightly.
4. Repeat to make the remaining 3 wraps.
   Serve immediately.

Nutritive values per wrap
Energy : 65 calories.
Protein : 3.4gm.
Carbohydrate : 9.1 gm.
Fat : 1.7 gm.
Vitamin A : 959.5 mcg.
Fibre : 1.2 mg.

· SPICY CHAPATI ·

Left-over chapatis when made like this taste delicious. For a healthier alternative, add a cupful of mixed boiled vegetables at step 3.

Preparation time : 2 minutes.   Cooking time : 7 minutes.   Serves 2.

left-over whole wheat chapatis approx. 200 mm. (8") in diameter, torn into pieces

Other ingredients
cups buttermilk (made with low fat curds (yoghurt), page 101)
2 tsp mustard seeds (rai)
tsp urad dal (split black lentils)
to 8 curry leaves
2 tsp turmeric powder (haldi)
tsp chilli powder
tsp grated jaggery (gur)
salt to taste
tsp oil

For the garnish
2 tbsp chopped coriander

1. Heat the oil in a non-stick pan and add the mustard seeds and urad dal.
2. When the mustard seeds crackle, add the curry leaves and the chapati pieces and sauté for ½ minute.
3. Add the buttermilk, turmeric powder, chilli powder, jaggery and salt and mix well.
4. Bring to a boil and serve hot garnished with the coriander.

Handy tip : To make 2 cups buttermilk, whisk together ¾ cup fresh low fat curds with 1¼ cup of water.

Nutritive values per serving
Energy : 193 calories.
Protein : 7.8 gm.
Carbohydrate : 33.2 gm.
Fat : 3. 2 gm.
Calcium : 128.7 mg.

· MASALA CHEESE TOAST ·

Picture on page 75

W hole wheat bread topped with vitamin A rich vegetables and calcium rich cheese... Just perfect to tickle your taste buds.

Preparation time : 15 minutes.   Cooking time : 5 minutes.   Makes 4 toasts.
Baking time : 5 minutes.   Baking temperature : 200°C (400°F).

slices whole wheat bread
tsp grated cheese

or the curry
cup finely chopped boiled vegetables (cabbage, cauliflower, green peas, french beans, apsicum)
cup potatoes, boiled and mashed lightly
tbsp finely chopped onions
tsp finely chopped green chillies
tsp chilli powder
pinches garam masala
tbsp chopped coriander

2 tsp oil
salt to taste

1. Heat the oil in a non-stick pan, add the onions and cook till the onions turn translucent.
2. Add the vegetables, potatoes, green chillies, chilli powder, garam masala, coriander and salt and cook for 1 or 2 minutes.
3. Remove and cool.
4. Toast the bread slices till they are slightly crisp.
5. Pour 2 tbsp of the mixture on each toast.
6. Top with a tsp of grated cheese.
7. Grill in a pre-heated oven approx. 200°C (400°F) till brown spots appear on the cheese. Serve hot.

Nutritive values per toast
Energy : 92 calories.
Protein : 2.8 gm.
Carbohydrate : 12.2 gm.
Fat : 3.6 gm.
Calcium : 34.9 mg.
Vitamin A : 152.6 mcg.

Masala Cheese Toast : Recipe on page 73 •

· BREAD BHURJI ·

*T*his recipe is an answer to a good, tasty breakfast entrée in a hurry which is enjoyed by people of all ages.

Preparation time : 5 minutes.   Cooking time : 9 minutes.   Serves 4.

10 slices whole wheat bread, cut into cubes
1 cup low fat curds (yoghurt), page 101
¼ tsp turmeric powder (haldi)
1 tsp cumin seeds (jeera)
1 green chilli, slit
3 to 4 curry leaves
1 tsp grated ginger
¼ cup onions, sliced
2 tsp oil
salt to taste

For the garnish
¼ cup coriander, chopped

In a bowl, combine the curds, turmeric powder and salt with 2 tbsp of water and mix well.

Add the cubes of bread and mix well till the bread is coated with the curd mixture.

Heat the oil in a non-stick pan and add the cumin seeds.

When they crackle, add the green chillies, curry leaves and ginger and sauté for a few seconds.

Add the onion slices and sauté till they are lightly browned.

Add the bread mixture and sauté over low heat, stirring occasionally till the bread browns lightly.

Serve hot garnished with the coriander.

utritive values per serving
ergy : 175 calories.
otein : 6.6 gm.
rbohydrate : 29.9 gm.
t : 3.2 gm.
lcium : 91.9 mg.

• STUFFED CURRY PARATHAS •

A classic satiating breakfast which makes use of any left-over subzi in your refrigerator. You can even knead the dough the previous day for mornings that you know will be busy.

Preparation time : 15 minutes.   Cooking time : 20 minutes.   Makes 6 parathas.

1 cup of any left-over sukhi subzi
3 tsp oil to cook

For the dough
2 cups wheat flour (gehun ka atta)
¼ cup low fat milk, page 101
salt to taste

For serving
low fat curds (yoghurt), page 101

For the dough

Mix all the ingredients required for the dough and add enough water to make a soft dough.

Knead the dough very well and keep aside for 15 minutes.

Divide the dough into 6 equal parts and roll out into rounds with the help of a little flour.

Cook each round very lightly on a non-stick pan and keep in a folded wet napkin.

How to proceed

Put 2 tbsp of the stuffing in the centre of each round and fold like an envelope from all corners.

Put the envelope on a non-stick pan with the open edges at the bottom. Cook for a few minutes using a little oil, turn over on the other side and cook again until crisp.

Repeat with the remaining rounds to make 5 more parathas.

Serve hot with low fat curds.

Nutritive values per paratha

Energy : 166 calories.

Protein : 5.0 gm.

Carbohydrate : 27.4 gm.

Fat : 4.0 gm.

Fibre : 0.8 gm.

· TOASTED ROTI ·

An imaginative way to turn plain left-over chapatis into a colourful and flavourful delicacy for a satiating breakfast.

Preparation time : 30 minutes.   Cooking time : 15 minutes.   Makes 8 rotis.

8 left-over whole wheat chapatis, approx. (200 mm. (8")) in diameter
2 tsp oil for greasing

For the mint stuffing
1 cup mint, finely chopped
2 green chillies, finely chopped
½ tsp salt
½ tsp amchur (dry mango powder)
1 tbsp dried bread crumbs

For serving
herb cheese, page 92

For the mint stuffing
Mix all the ingredients well.

How to proceed

1. Place a chapati on a flat surface. Put a portion of the stuffing on it and fold into a semi-circle.
2. Grease the outer surface with oil and put in a bread toaster.
3. Toast till chapati is crisp and brown spots appear on each side.
4. Cut into strips and serve immediately.

Handy tip : You may use different stuffings in this recipe. Here are a few suggestions.

VARIATION 1 : SPINACH STUFFING

3 cups spinach (palak), finely chopped
1 cup onions, chopped
2 green chillies, chopped
4 tbsp crumbled low fat paneer (cottage cheese), page 102
2 tsp oil
salt to taste

1. Heat the oil and fry the onions for ½ minute. Add the green chillies and fry again for a few seconds.
2. Add the spinach and cook for 2 minutes.
3. Drain the water if any.
4. Add the paneer and salt. Mix well.

VARIATION 2: CAULIFLOWER AND METHI STUFFING

2 cups cauliflower, grated
½ tsp cumin seeds (jeera)
½ cup onions, chopped
2 green chillies, chopped
2 tbsp chopped fenugreek (methi) leaves
½ tsp chopped ginger
2 tsp oil
salt to taste

1. Heat the oil and fry the cumin seeds until they crackle.
2. Add the onion, green chillies and ginger and fry again for ½ minute.
3. Add the cauliflower and salt, sprinkle a little water and cook until three quarter's cooked.
4. Add the fenugreek leaves and mix well.

Nutritive values per roti
Energy : 82 calories.
Protein : 2.6 gm.
Carbohydrate : 14.3 gm.
Fat : 1.6 gm.
Vitamin A : 77.9 mcg.

· COOKED RICE PANCAKES ·

*W*hip up these delicious pancakes in a jiffy.

Preparation time : 10 minutes.   Cooking time : 20 minutes.   Makes 10 pancakes.

2 cups cooked rice
1/3 cup carrot, grated
1/3 cup spring onions, chopped
1/3 cup cabbage, shredded
1/4 cup whole wheat flour (gehun ka atta)
1/2 cup Bengal gram flour (besan)
1/2 tsp turmeric powder (haldi)
1/4 tsp asafoetida (hing)
2 green chillies, finely chopped
2 tbsp low fat curds (yoghurt), page 101
2 tbsp chopped coriander
salt to taste

Other ingredients
1 tsp oil to cook

83

For serving
nutritious green chutney, page 98

1. Combine the ingredients except the oil in a bowl.
2. Add enough water to make a soft dough.
3. Divide the dough into 10 equal portions.
4. Using wet hands, press one portion of the dough onto a damp cloth to form a 100 mm. (4") diameter circle.
5. Lift the cloth and upturn the pancake on to a non-stick pan.
6. Cook on both sides till golden brown using a little oil. Repeat with the remaining dough to make 9 more pancakes.
   Serve hot with the nutritious green chutney.

Nutritive values per pancake
Energy : 81 calories.
Protein : 1.8 gm.
Carbohydrate : 11.5 gm.
Fat : 3.0 gm.
Vitamin A : 138.8 mcg.

Butter Substitutes : Clockwise from top to bottom →
Parsley Yoghurt Spread : Recipe on page 94,
Chunky Vegetable Spread : Recipe on page 93 and
Herb Cheese : Recipe on page 92

· FRE/H COMPLEXION EXPRE// ·

Picture on page 1

A *healthy pineapple, cucumber and apple drink.*

Preparation time : 2 minutes.   No cooking.   Makes 1 glass.

2 slices pineapple, with skin
½ medium cucumber, peeled
½ apple, deseeded

1. Cut the pineapple, cucumber and apple into big pieces.
2. Push pineapple through hopper (juicer) with cucumber and apple for a healthy drink. Serve immediately.

Handy tip : If you do not have a juicer, just blend all ingredients in a mixer using half a cup of water and then strain.

Nutritive values for 1 glass

Energy : 60 calories.	Protein : 0.4 gm.	Carbohydrate : 13.5 gm.
Fat : 0.4 gm.	Vitamin C : 8.4 mg.	

· HERBAL CAFFEINE-FREE TEA ·

O therwise known as tulsi tea. The tulsi plant is venerated by Hindus and its leaves are also used in religious ceremonies.

Preparation time : a few minutes.   Boiling time : 2 minutes.   Serves 4.

¼ cup tulsi leaves
4 tsp jaggery (gur)
1 tbsp lemon juice

1. Blend the tulsi leaves and jaggery in a blender.
2. Boil 1½ cups of water.
3. Add the jaggery mixture and lemon juice to the boiling water. Strain. Serve hot.

Nutritive values per serving
Energy : 32 calories.
Protein : 0.2 gm.
Carbohydrate : 7.4 gm.
Fat : 0.1 gm.

• PAPAYA MANGO SMOOTHIE •

Picture on page 1

If you do not have the time for an elaborate breakfast don't forget to have a smoothie. It is sure to sustain until lunch.

Preparation time : a few minutes.   No cooking.   Makes 2 glasses.

1 cup papaya purée
1 cup fresh mango pulp
1 tbsp sugar (optional)
1 tbsp lemon juice (optional)
crushed ice

1. Blend all the ingredients except the ice in the mixer.
2. Pour into individual glasses.
    Serve with crushed ice.

Nutritive values per glass
Energy : 74 calories.
Protein : 0.8 gm.
Carbohydrate : 16.9 gm.
Fat : 0.4 gm.
Vitamin A : 1238.6 mcg.

• TOMATO APPLE DRINK •

Picture on page 1

Cool and delicious vitamin A and fibre relish.

Preparation time : 10 minutes.   No cooking.   Makes 2 glasses.

cup apple, chopped
cup tomatoes, chopped
tsp honey
to 6 ice cubes

Blanch the tomatoes in hot water 2 to 3 minutes.
Remove and cut into pieces.
Add the apple and honey and blend in a blender with 1 cup of water till it is smooth.
Do not strain.
Pour into 2 glasses and serve immediately.

utritive values per glass
nergy : 45 calories.
otein : 0.9 gm.
arbohydrate : 9.9 gm.
t : 0.3 gm.
bre : 1.0 gm.
tamin A : 273.8 mcg.

89

· HEALTH DRINK ·

Picture on page 1

*T*his tomato, carrot and orange combination is rich in Vitamin A and hence good for the eye.

Preparation time : a few minutes.　　No cooking.　　Makes 2 glasses.

1 cup tomatoes, chopped
1 cup carrot, chopped
segments of 1 orange
a few drops lemon juice
1 tsp sugar
salt and pepper to taste
crushed ice to serve

1. Mix the tomatoes, carrot, orange, lemon juice, sugar and ½ cup of water and blend in a blender of obtain juice. Strain.
2. Add the salt and pepper.
   Serve cold with crushed ice.

Nutritive values per glass
Energy : 66 calories.
Protein : 1.4 gm.
Carbohydrate : 14.3 gm.
Fat : 0.3 gm.
Vitamin A : 1388.1 mcg.

PINEAPPLE SWEET LIME DRINK

Picture on page 1

The micronutrient rich subza complement this sweet and sour drink perfectly.

Preparation time : 5 minutes.   Makes 2 glasses.

4 slices pineapple, with skin
2 cups sweet lime segments, chopped
½ tsp subza (garden cress seeds)
¼ cup crushed ice

1. Soak the subza seeds in water for 5 minutes.
2. Push the pineapple and sweet lime segments through a hopper.
3. Pour into individual glasses over crushed ice.
4. Garnish with the subza seeds.
   Serve immediately.

Nutritive values per glass
Energy : 99 calories.
Protein : 1.8 gm.
Carbohydrate : 21.2 gm.
Fat : 0.8 gm.
Iron : 3.2 mg.

BUTTER SUBSTITUTES

Relish these butter substitutes as bread spreads or as accompaniments to your favourite dish.

• HERB CHEESE •

Picture on page 85

Preparation time : 4 minutes.   No cooking.   Serves 2.

¾ cup low fat paneer (cottage cheese), page 102, grated
1 tbsp low fat curds (yoghurt), page 101
1 tbsp chopped parsley / coriander
½ tsp chopped dill (shepu)
1 clove garlic, grated
1 green chilli, chopped
salt to taste

1. Combine all the ingredients in a mixer and blend till smooth.
2. Spread over plastic film and roll into a cylinder of 37 mm. (1½") diameter.
3. Refrigerate till firm. Unwrap the plastic film and cut into thick slices.

Nutritive values per serving
Energy : 119 calories.
Protein : 12.7 gm.
Carbohydrate : 17.1 gm.
Fat : 0 gm.
Calcium : 458.1 gm.

· CHUNKY VEGETABLE SPREAD ·

Picture on page 85

BUTTER
SUBSTITUTES

Preparation time : 15 minutes.   No cooking.   Makes 1½ cups (approx. 21 tbsp).

2 tbsp low fat milk, page 101
¼ cup low fat paneer (cottage cheese), page 101 grated
2 tbsp chopped celery
¼ cup carrots, chopped
¼ cup capsicum, chopped
2 tbsp chopped spring onion greens
2 tbsp chopped tomatoes
¼ cup cucumber, chopped
1 tbsp chopped parsley
salt to taste

Combine all ingredients in a bowl. Chill for 2 hours and use as required.

Nutritive values per tbsp
Energy : 13 calories.
Protein : 1.3 gm.
Carbohydrate : 1.9 gm.
Fat : 0 gm.
Calcium : 48.9 mg.

· PARSLEY YOGHURT SPREAD ·

Picture on page 85

Preparation time : 15 minutes.   No cooking.   Makes 1 cup (approx. 14 tbsp).

1 cup low fat curds (yoghurt), page 101
1 tbsp finely chopped parsley
1 tbsp finely chopped spring onion greens
1½ tsp finely chopped garlic
salt to taste

1. Hang the curds in a muslin cloth for 15 to 20 minutes till it is thick.
2. Add all the other ingredients to this hung curd and blend in a mixer till it is smooth.
   Serve chilled.

Nutritive values per tbsp

Energy : 10 calories.	Protein : 0.7 gm.	Carbohydrate : 1.7 gm.
Fat : 0 gm.	Vitamin A : 109.8 mcg.	

· GARLIC TOMATO CHUTNEY ·

Preparation time : 10 minutes.   Cooking time : 15 minutes.
Makes ¾ cup (approx.11 tbsp).

6 to 8 large cloves garlic, finely chopped

¼ cup spring onion whites, chopped
tbsp spring onion greens, finely chopped
dry red chilies, soaked
cup tomatoes, finely chopped
tbsp finely chopped coriander
tsp olive oil or oil
alt to taste

. Drain the soaked chillies and chop them finely.
. Heat the oil, add the spring onion whites and garlic and sauté over a slow flame for
  4 to 5 minutes till they are lightly brown.
. Add the chillies and salt and sauté again.
. Add the tomatoes and cook for 10 to 12 minutes over a slow flame till the tomatoes
  are soft and can be mashed lightly.
. Cool completely and add the coriander and spring onion greens and mix well.
  Serve chilled or at room temperature.

utritive values per tbsp
nergy : 9 calories.
rotein : 0.2 gm.
arbohydrate : 0.9 gm.
at : 0.5 gm.
itamin A : 74.1 mcg.

· CORIANDER GARLIC CHUTNEY ·

Preparation time : 5 minutes.   No cooking.   Makes ½ cup (approx. 7 tbsp).

½ cup fresh green garlic, chopped (including the greens)
1 cup coriander, finely chopped
1 tsp lemon juice
1 tbsp roasted Bengal gram (daria)
½ cup water
salt to taste

Grind all the ingredients together in a blender to get a smooth chutney.
Store refrigerated.

Nutritive values per tbsp

Energy : 10 calories.	Protein : 0.6 gm.	Carbohydrate : 1.8 gm.
Fat : 0.2 gm.	Vitamin C : 2.9 mg.	

· HIGH FIBRE CHUTNEY ·

Preparation time : 5 minutes.   No Cooking.   Makes 1 cup (approx. 14 tbsp).

½ cup green peas, boiled
1 cup chopped coriander
1 to 2 green chillies
2 large cloves garlic
25 mm. (1") piece ginger

uice of ½ lemon
1 tsp sugar
salt to taste

1. Combine all the ingredients in a blender and grind to a fine paste using approx.
   2 tbsp water.
2. Refrigerate in an air-tight container and use as required.

Nutritive values per tbsp

Energy : 7 calories.   Protein : 0.4 gm.   Carbohydrate : 1.3 gm.
Fat : 0 gm.   Fibre : 0.2 gm.

· CARROT GARLIC CHUTNEY ·

BUTTER
SUBSTITUTES

Preparation time : 30 minutes.   No cooking.   Makes ½ cup (approx. 7 tbsp).

cup carrots, thickly grated
tbsp garlic, chopped
tsp chilli powder
4 tsp lemon juice
tsp oil
tsp salt

Grind the garlic, chilli powder, lemon juice and salt to a fine paste in a blender.
Combine the carrots, garlic paste and oil in a bowl and mix well. Serve immediately.

Nutritive values per tbsp

Energy : 13 calories.   Protein : 0.1 gm.   Carbohydrate : 1.4 gm.
Fat : 0.7 gm.   Vitamin A : 244.0 mcg.

· NUTRITIOUJ GREEN CHUTNEY ·

Preparation time : 10 minutes.   No cooking.   Makes 1 cup (approx. 14 tbsp).

2 cups mint (phudina) leaves, chopped
1 cup coriander, chopped
¾ cup onions, sliced
juice of 1 to 2 lemons
1 tsp sugar
4 to 6 green chillies
salt to taste

Combine all the ingredients and grind to a smooth paste in a blender using very little water. Refrigerate and use as required.

Nutritive values per tbsp

Energy : 46 calories.   Protein : 2.5 gm.   Carbohydrate : 7.2 gm.
Fat : 0.8 gm.   Folic acid : 17.9 mcg.

SALT SUBSTITUTES

Kiss your salt cellars goodbye.
These natural herb and spice blends are all set to win your heart over.

· SESAME AND HERB BLEND ·

Preparation time : a few minutes.   No cooking.   Makes ⅓ cup.

tsp dehydrated onion flakes or onion powder
½ tsp garlic powder
tsp sesame seeds (til), lightly roasted
Kashmiri chillies, lightly roasted
tsp oregano
pinches citric acid (nimbu ke phool)
2 tsp salt (optional)

Mix all the ingredients and blend in a blender. Store in an air-tight container and use as required.

· GARDEN DILL BLEND ·

Preparation time : a few minutes.   No cooking.   Makes ⅓ cup.

tsp dehydrated onion flakes or onion powder

2 tsp garlic powder
4½ tsp dried dill (shepu)
½ tsp white pepper powder
3 pinches citric acid (nimbu ke phool)
½ tsp salt (optional)

Mix all the ingredients and blend in a blender. Store in an air-tight container and use as required.

· SPICY MEXICAN BLEND ·

Preparation time : a few minutes.   No cooking.   Makes ⅓ cup.

6 tsp dehydrated onion flakes or onion powder
1½ tsp garlic powder
2 tsp roasted cumin (jeera) powder
2 tsp chilli powder
1 tsp coriander-cumin seed (dhania-jeera) powder
4 Kashmiri chillies, roasted
2 pinches citric acid (nimbu ke phool)
½ tsp salt (optional)

Mix all the ingredients and blend in a blender. Store in an air-tight container and use as required.

BASIC RECIPES

LOW FAT MILK

Preparation time : 5 minutes.   Cooking time : 7 minutes.   Makes 1 litre (5 cups).

00 grams skim milk powder, 1 litre water

. Mix the skim milk powder in 1½ cups of water and make a smooth paste.
. Add the remaining water and mix with a whisk. Boil and use as required.

Nutritive values per cup
nergy : 71 calories.   Protein : 7.6 gm.   Carbohydrate : 10.2 gm.
at : 0 gm.   Calcium : 274.0 mg.

LOW FAT CURDS

Preparation time : 5 cups.   No cooking.   Makes 5 cups.

litre low fat milk, recipe above
tbsp curds (made the previous day)

Warm the milk.
Add the curds, mix well and cover.

3. Keep aside until the curds ser (approx. 5 to 6 hours). During the cold climate, place inside a cupboard or a closed oven for setting.

Nutritive values per cup

Energy : 71 calories. Protein : 7.6 gm. Carbohydrate : 10.2 gm.
Fat : 0 gm. Calcium : 274.0 mg.

LOW FAT PANEER

Preparation time : 30 minutes. Cooking time : 10 minutes. Makes 100 grams.

2 cups low fat milk, page 101
1 cup low fat curds, page 101, beaten

1. Put the milk to boil in a broad pan. When it starts boiling, add the low fat curds and mix well.
2. Remove from the heat and stir gently until the milk curdles.
3. Strain and tie the curdled milk in a muslin cloth. Hang for about half an hour to allow the whey to drain out and use as required.

Handy tip : If you want firm paneer, cover the block with a heavy weight to compress the paneer. This way you will be able to cut cubes from the paneer.

Nutritive values for ¾ cup

Energy : 214 calories. Protein : 22.8 gm. Carbohydrate : 30.6 gm.
Fat : 0.1 gm. Calcium : 822.0 mg.

by Tarla Dalal

The Total Health series is a range of cookbooks specially designed and carefully researched by a team of qualified nutritionists. These books are an action-oriented guide for good health and wellness to suit the nutritional needs for different age groups, be it an expectant mum, a baby, an individual who has a medical problem or aims to lose weight. These books will help you and your family stay in fine fettle. They have opened new vistas in the field of cooking while providing you with healthy guidelines for adding verve and vitality to your life. Some of the titles in this series are:

Low Calorie Healthy Cooking

Pregnancy Cook Book

Baby & Toddler Cook Book